Heavenly and Beginner-friendly

Cake Recipes

By: Les Ilagan

No part of this book may be reproduced, scanned, or distributed in any printed or electronic form without permission. Please do not participate or encourage piracy of copyrighted materials in violation of the author's rights. Purchase only authorized editions.

Copyright © by Les Ilagan

All Rights Reserved

Les Ilagan

Copyright © CONTENT ARCADE PUBLISHING. All rights reserved.

This cookbook is copyright protected and meant for personal use only.

No part of this cookbook may be used, paraphrased, reproduced, scanned, distributed or sold in any printed or electronic form without permission of the author and the publishing company. Copying pages or any part of this book for any purpose other than own personal use is prohibited and would also mean violation of copyright law.

DISCLAIMER

Content Arcade Publishing and its authors are joined together in their efforts in creating these pages and their publications. Content Arcade Publishing and its authors make no assurance of any kind, stated or implied, with respect to the information provided.

LIMITS OF LIABILITY

Content Arcade Publishing and its authors shall not be held legally responsible in the event of incidental or consequential damages in line with, or arising out of, the supplying of the information presented here.

TABLE OF CONTENTS

DISCLAIMER.............................3

Introduction....................................6

Chocolate Cakes............................13

Hershey's Ultimate Chocolate CakeRecipe 13

Cadbury Chocolate Cake Recipe........... 20

Easy Raspberry Chocolate Cake Recipe 23

Dark Chocolate Mousse CakeRecipe ... 26

Flourless Choco Cake Recipe 29

Yummy Tiramisu CakeRecipe 35

Chocolate Cakewith Coffee Mascarpone Recipe 38

BittersweetChocolate CakeRecipe 44

Mom's Awesome Chocolate CakeRecipe 53

Strawberry Mascarpone Cream Cake Recipe 62

Mango Ricotta Cheesecake Recipe 68

Cake Recipes

Mini Ring Cake with Ricotta and Raspberry Recipe 88

Sweet Apple Cake with WalnutsRecipe 91

Simple Coffee CakeRecipe 93

INTRODUCTION

This book gives you a collection of delicious cake recipes that you can do at home. There are also cake recipes in this book that allows you to have something special to serve your family and friends.

The ingredients used are not hard to find. In fact, you can buy the ingredients in your nearest grocery or supermarket. Furthermore, common household measurements were used in the recipes to enable you to do your homemade cake easily.

As a general rule, whatever type of cake you are making, be sure to follow closely the recipe. When you bake cakes, it is always necessary to execute the right method as well as take into consideration the order and measurement of ingredients. The latter really counts when baking cakes.

This recipe book is divided into different types of cakes such as Chocolate cakes, Cakes with fruits, Coffee cakes, Tea cakes, and Chiffon cakes. So you will have more recipes to choose from.

You will surely enjoy baking these 50 beginner-friendly and delicious cake recipes!!

Do's And Don'ts Of Making The Perfect Cake

Baking is can be considered as a science, you need to measure everything accurately like the ingredients, baking time, number of mixing times, and the oven temperatureto be able to come up with beautiful and great tasting cake.

Here are some tips to guide you before you bake that special cake for your loved ones:

1. It is important to pre-heat your oven.
It is necessary to know your oven well. You need to get yourself an oven thermometer to know if your oven is calibrated accurately. In addition, you also need to bake your cake in the middle of the oven because too close to the top or bottom can result to overbrowning and dry cake.

2. Choose the right size of pan for your cake

Always remember that the pan size is important. In every cake recipe, it is always specified what type and size of pan you will need to bake your cake. This is true because the cake increases in volume for about 50 to 100% during baking.

3. To be able to butter or grease the pan properly, use a pastry brush or an oil spray as it will increase coverage of the baking pan.

4. Make sure to use certain ingredients such as butter, milk and eggs when they are <u>at room temperature</u> otherwise the mixture will not properly emulsify.

5. You have to choose correctly the type of flour you will use for your cake because different types of flour have varying percentages of protein. The more protein you have in your cake, the more gluten you have. Cake flour gives you extra light

baked goods. Bread flour for denser cakes while all-purpose flour can yield tender cakes.

6. Measure the flour properly. Spoon the flour into a measuring cup to be accurate in measuring the flour.

7.Use the best ingredients when baking your cake. Choose high quality when buying your ingredients.

8.Avoid over mixing the batter.
The mixing times is important because the length of mixing will determine how much gluten in the flour will likely develop. You will destroy some of the air bubbles if you have over-mixed the batter. Likewise, do not under mix the batter. Inadequate gluten will prevent the cake from setting correctly or forming a rigid structure resulting to a crumbly and flaky cake. To ensure proper mixing, beat cake batter on low speed until the ingredients are <u>just combined</u>.

9.Avoid constantly opening the oven's door
If you accidentally open the door of the oven during the baking process, it will result to a dense cake. Because varying oven temperature is very crucial when baking a cake.

10.Put your prepared pan at the center of the rack and set in the middle of the oven.

11. Don't leave the cake on the pan.
You can cool the cake on the pan for a few minutes before you turn them onto a wire rack. If not stated in the recipe instruction, do not leave the cake on the pan for too long because the heat from the pan can cause the cake to overcook or can eventually dry your cake.

12. In choosing a cake filling, make sure that the ingredients for the cake filling you have chosen will complement the flavor of the cake. Also, must ensure that the filling is stable to hold up to the cake

otherwise your cake might become soggy if it has runny texture.

13. When frosting your cake, the usual frosting or icing that you can use are buttercream, fluffy frosting or dusted icing sugar.

13. It is best to cool the cake upside down on a wire rack.

14. Always remember that most pound cakes get their fine and soft texture and desired moistness by first creaming together fat and sugar, then add eggs and slowly incorporate the dry ingredients into the mixture while alternating with a liquid such as milk.

15. Angel, sponge, or chiffon cake can get their foamy like airy texture when egg whites are beaten until becomes voluminous then folded into a batter or flour mixture.

CHOCOLATE CAKES

Hershey's Ultimate Chocolate Cake Recipe

This seems to be the best chocolate cake recipe ever!!

Preparation Time: 20minutes
Total Time: 55 minutes
Yield:12 servings

Ingredients
¾ cup Hershey's powdered cocoa
2 cups brown sugar

1 ¾ cups all-purpose flour
1 ½ tsp. baking powder
1 ½ tsp. baking soda
1 tsp. salt
1 cup whole milk
½ cup vegetable oil
2 medium eggs
2 tsp. pure vanilla extract
1 cup boiling water
Cooking oil spray
Hershey's Milk Chocolate bar, shaved, to serve

Chocolate frosting:
½ cup (1 stick) salted butter
2 ½ cups powdered sugar
2/3 cup Hershey's powdered cocoa
1/3 cup whole milk
1 tsp.pure vanilla extract

Method
1. Preheat oven to 350F.
2. Grease two 9-inch round baking pans with oil spray. Sprinkle with some flour.
3. Mix together cocoa, sugar, flour, baking powder, baking soda and salt in a large mixing bowl. Add milk, vegetable oil, eggs and

vanilla. Beat the mixture on a medium speed of mixer for 2 minutes. Then, stir in boiling water. Divide the batter evenly between the two prepared pans and spread evenly.
4. Bake for 30 to 35 minutes in the oven or until a toothpick inserted into the cake comes out clean. Cool cake completely in pans on wire racks.
5. *To make Chocolate frosting:* Using a mixer, cream butter with cocoa in a large mixing bowl, gradually add powdered sugar alternately with milk. Add the vanilla extract and beat on high for 1 minute.
6. Frost the cake with the delicious chocolate frosting. Sprinkle with chocolate shavings.
7. Serve and enjoy.

Les Ilagan

Decadent Chocolate Cake Recipe

This chocolate cake smells and tastes great. You will love each slice of it!

Preparation Time: 45 minutes
Total Time: 2 hours and 45 minutes
Yield: 12 servings

Ingredients
1 cup powdered cocoa
1 cup plain flour
2 cups self-raising flour
2 cups caster sugar

½ tsp. bicarbonate of soda
6 medium eggs
10 oz. butter
1 ¾ cups milk
Cooking oil spray

Chocolate Butter Icing:
8oz. butter, sliced into cubes
1 ½ cups pure icing sugar, sifted
8 oz. dark chocolate, melted and cooled

Method

1. Preheat oven to 300 F. Grease a 10-inch round pan with oil spray. Put a non-stick baking paper on the base and sides of the pan.
2. Mix together the cocoa, plain flour, self-raising flour, sugar, baking soda, butter, egg, and milk in a large mixing bowl. Beat on a low speed for about 30 seconds using an electric mixer.
3. Adjust the speed to high and beat further 1 to 2 minutes or until the mixture is thick and mixed thoroughly. Put the mixture into the prepared pan and spread evenly.

4. Bake in preheated oven for 2 hours or until a toothpick inserted into the cake comes out clean. Remove from the oven. Cool for 10 minutes and turn onto a wire rack until completely cool.
5. *To make the Chocolate Butter Icing:* Put the butter in a large bowl. Beat for 2 minutes using an electric mixer. Slowly and gradually add the icing sugar and beat until the mixture looks light and fluffy.
6. Add the melted chocolate. Stir together very rapidly until smooth and well combined.
7. *To assemble the cake:* Trim the top to make the surface even. Split the cake horizontally into 3 even layers. Invert top layer on a cake stand. Spread a thick layer of icing over the cake layer. Then, top with another layer of cake and spread more icing onto the cake. Repeat procedure for the last cake layer. Spread the remaining icing over the top and sides of the cake

using a spatula. Smooth the chocolate icing.
8. Serve and enjoy.

Cadbury Chocolate Cake Recipe

This is a great chocolate cake recipe for all Cadbury chocolate lovers out there!

Preparation Time: 35 minutes
Total Time: 1 hour and 45 minutes
Yield: 8-10 servings

Ingredients

6oz. dark chocolate, roughly sliced or chopped
6 oz. unsalted butter
¾ cup caster sugar
4 large eggs
1 cup almond meal

1 cup self-raising flour, sifted
1 tsp. baking powder, sifted
½ cup whole milk
2 Cadbury Flake chocolate bars, crumbled
Cooking oil spray

Chocolate Cream:
1 ½ cup thick cream
6 oz.Cadbury milk chocolate, roughly chopped

Method

1. Preheat oven to 325 F. Grease a 9-inch round cake pan with oil spray.
2. Put the chocolate in a bowl over a pan of boiling water until chocolate has totally melted. Stir the chocolate until melted and smooth. Set aside.
3. Mix together the butter and sugar in a bowl. Beat with an electric mixer for 5 minutes or until the mixture turns light in color. Add eggs gradually or one at a time, beating thoroughly after each addition.

4. Stir in almond meal, flour, baking powder, milk and melted chocolate.
5. Place the mixture onto the prepared cake pan and bake for about 45 minutes or until a toothpick inserted into the cake comes out clean. Allow to cool for 10 minutes. Then, turn the cake in a wire rack to cool completely.
6. *To make the Chocolate Cream:* Heat cream over a low heat. Stir in chocolate until melted. Chill for about 15 minutes or until thick but still spreadable.
7. Spread cream over cake and sprinkle with Cadbury flakes bar on top.
8. Serve and enjoy.

Tip: You can double this recipe to make 2-3 layers of this awesome cake.

Easy Raspberry Chocolate Cake Recipe

If you don't have much time to prepare, try this chocolate cake recipe with raspberries!

Preparation Time: 20 minutes
Total Time: 60 minutes
Yield: 10 servings

Ingredients
6 oz. fresh raspberries
1 box Super Moist Chocolate Cake mix
½ cup butter
2 medium eggs
1 cup whole milk

½ cup sour cream
Cooking oil spray

Ganache:
¾ cup thick cream
1 Tbsp. butter
8 oz. bittersweet chocolate, roughly chopped

Method
1. Preheat oven to 350 F. Grease a 10-inch ringcake pan with oil spray.
2. Combine the cake mix, eggs, milk and sour cream until just combined using an electric mixer.
3. Pour the mixture onto prepared cake pan. Bake for 50-60 minutes or until a toothpick inserted into the cake comes out clean. Cool in pan for 10 minutes. Turn the cake upside down on the wire rack to cool completely.
4. *To make the Ganache:* Heat cream and butter over a low heat. Add chocolate and stir until melted.

5. Pour ganache on top of the cake. Place raspberries at the center of the cake.
6. Serve and enjoy.

Dark Chocolate Mousse Cake Recipe

This is simply irresistible! The fresh berries adds a nice touch to this fantastic dessert or snack.

Preparation Time: 20 minutes
Total Time: 60 minutes
Yield: 10 servings

Ingredients
6 oz. plain chocolate biscuits

1/3 cup butter, melted
16 oz. dark chocolate, roughly chopped
2 cups thickened cream
¼ cup coffee flavored liqueur
Cocoa powder to dust
Fresh berries, to serve
Cooking oil spray

Method
1. Grease a 9-inch springform pan with oil spray.
2. Place the biscuits in a food processor. Process until biscuits become fine like breadcrumbs. Add the butter and process until combined well. Press the mixture onto base of the prepared pan. Refrigerate for 30 minutes.
3. Place the chocolate in a large heat proof bowl and place over a saucepan of simmering water. Stir for 10 minutes until melted and smooth. Remove from heat. Cool for 10-15 minutes.
4. Beat cream, liqueur using an electric mixer until soft peaks form. Fold cream mixture into chocolate. Pour the chocolate

mixture on top of the biscuit crust on the pan. Smooth using a spatula. Refrigerate for at least 4 hours.
5. Dust with cocoa powder.
6. Serve and enjoy.

Flourless Choco Cake Recipe

This is a great chocolate cake with a twist, almondsare used to replace flour in this recipe.

Preparation Time: 20 minutes
Total Time: 1 hour 15 minutes
Yield: 10 servings

Ingredients
6 oz. slivered almonds
4 oz. butter, chopped
6 oz. dark chocolate, chopped
2 Tbsp. freshly brewed black coffee

1/3 cup cocoa powder
¾ cup caster sugar
5 medium eggs, separated
Cocoa powder, to serve
Pure cream, to serve
Cooking oil spray

Method
1. Preheat oven to 350 F. Grease a 9-inchspringform cake pan with oil spray.
2. Put the almonds on a tray and bake for 5 to 10 minutes or until light golden in color. Cool completely. Put the almonds in a food processor. Process until finely chopped.
3. Combine butter, chocolate and coffee in a heat proof, microwave-safe bowl. Put bowl in the microwave, cook uncovered on medium-high for 2 to 3 minutes. Stir every minute or until almost smooth.
4. Add cocoa powder and whisk until smooth.
5. Add the egg yolks, half cup of sugar and almonds. Stir until combined.

6. Beat egg white using an electric mixer until soft peak forms. Add the remaining ¼ cup sugar, 1 tablespoon at a time, beating constantly until thick.
7. Fold the meringue (egg white mixture) onto the chocolate mixture.
8. Pour and spread the mixture into prepared pan. Bake for 40 to 45 minutes.
9. Cool cake completely in the pan.
10. Put a slice of cake on a plate. Dust with cocoa.
11. Serve and enjoy.

Flourless Hazelnut Chocolate Cake Recipe

This chocolate cake with hazelnut is so easy to make, moist and rich in flavor.

Preparation Time: 20 minutes
Total Time: 1 hour 30 minutes
Yield: 10 servings

Ingredients
8 oz. dark chocolate, roughly chopped
½ cup butter, cut into small pieces
2/3 cup caster sugar
6 medium egg yolks
6 medium egg whites

1 ½ cups hazelnut meal
Whipped cream, to serve
Cooking oil spray

Chocolate Icing:
10 oz. dark chocolate, chopped
2/3 cup heavy cream

Method
1. Preheat oven to 350. Grease a 9-inch round cake pan with oil spray.
2. Combine butter and chocolate in a saucepan over low heat. Stir until melted. Set aside to cool slightly.
3. Place sugar and eggyolks in a bowl. Beat until creamy and thick using an electric mixer until combined well. Add hazelnut meal. Beat to combine.
4. Put the eggwhites in a bowl. Beat using an electric mixer until soft peaks form. Stir one third of eggwhites into chocolate mixture using a metal spoon. Gently fold remaining eggwhites to the chocolate mixture. Pour in the prepared pan and bake for 40-50 minutes or until tested done. Cool in wire rack.

5. *To make Chocolate Icing:* Put chocolate and cream in a saucepan over low heat. Cook, stirring constantly for 3 to 4 minutes or until smooth. Spread on top and the sides of the cake.
6. Top with whipped cream.
7. Serve and enjoy.

Cake Recipes

Yummy Tiramisu Cake Recipe

This is a delicious tiramisu cake recipe. Your loved ones will surely enjoy each and every bite!

Preparation Time: 30 minutes
Total Time: 1 hour 30 minutes
Yield: 10 servings

Ingredients
2 cups fresh ricotta cheese
¼ cup coffee flavored liqueur
¼ cup powdered sugar
4 oz. dark chocolate, finely sliced

½ (16 oz.) packaged double sponge cake, no filling
½ cup espresso coffee, cooled
2/3 cup icing sugar mixture
2 Tbsp. cocoa powder, sifted
1 Tbsp. unsalted butter, softened
3 Tbsp. whole milk
Powdered cocoa, to serve
Shaved dark chocolate, to serve

Method

1. Using a mixer, beat ricotta, liqueur, and sugar for 2 minutes or until mixture becomes smooth. Stir in chocolate. Set aside.
2. Cut cake horizontally into thirds using a serrated knife. Put the base on a plate. Brush with espresso. Spread with ½ of the ricotta. Put the middle layer of the cake, brush with espresso. Spread with the remaining ricotta mixture. Brush cut side of sponge top with coffee. Put over ricotta mixture, cut side down.
3. Mix together icing sugar and cocoa in a bowl. Make a well in the center. Gradually stir in butter and

milk until combined. Spread over cake. Chill for 3 to 4 hours.
4. Sprinkle with cocoa powder and chocolate shavings.
5. Serve and enjoy.

Chocolate Cake With Coffee Mascarpone Recipe

This is an amazing chocolate cake recipe. You can serve this during special occasions.

Preparation Time: 30 minutes
Total Time: 60 minutes
Yield: 6-8 servings

Ingredients

16 oz. dark chocolate, roughly chopped
½ cup (1 stick) unsalted butter
2 Tbsp. honey
4 large eggs

1 Tbsp. powdered sugar
¼ cup all-purpose flour, sifted
Cooking oil spray
Fresh mint leaves, to serve

Coffee Mascarpone:
2 Tbsp. instant coffee + 2 Tbsp. boiling water
1 cup mascarpone cheese
2 Tbsp. pure icing sugar

Method

1. Preheat oven to 400 F. Grease a 9-inch round spring form cake pan with oil spray.
2. In a bowl, melt the chocolate, butter and honey over a saucepan of simmering water. Set aside and allow to cool.
3. In a large bowl, combinethe eggs and sugar. Beat on high using an electric mixer for 10 minutes until very thick and light in color. Stir in the flour then fold ontothe chocolate mixture until combined well. Pour the mixture in the prepared cake pan.Bake in the middle shelf of the oven for about

10-15 minutes. Remove from oven and run a knife on the edge of the cake. Refrigerate cake for at least 2 hours.

4. *To make the Coffee Mascarpone:* dissolve coffee in a 2 tablespoons of boiling water. Set aside to cool. Using an electric mixer. Beat together coffee,mascarpone and sugar in a bowl until stiff.
5. Slice and serve the cake with a dollop of coffee mascarpone. Garnish with fresh mint leaves.
6. Enjoy.

Amazing Dark Chocolate Cake Recipe

This chocolate cake recipe has a moist texture and dark chocolate flavor.

Preparation Time: 30 minutes
Total Time: 1 hour and 20 minutes
Yield: 10-12 servings

Ingredients

2 cups boiling water
1 ¼ cup unsweetened cocoa powder
2 tsp. baking soda
2 ¾ cup all-purpose flour
2 tsp. baking powder

½ tsp. salt
1 cup unsalted butter, softened
2 ¼ cups white sugar
4 large eggs
1 ½ tsp. vanilla extract
Cooking oil spray
Fresh berries, to serve

Dark Chocolate Icing:
16 oz. dark chocolate, roughly chopped
1½ cup heavy cream

Method

1. Preheat oven to 350 F. Grease three 9-inch round cake pans with oil spray.
2. Pour boiling water over cocoa in a medium bowl. Whisk until smooth. Cool the mixture.
3. Sift together the dry ingredients (baking soda, flour, baking powder, and salt). Set aside.
4. Using an electric mixer, cream butter and sugar together in a large bowl until fluffy and light in color. Gradually add eggs or one at a time then stir in vanilla extract. Add the flour mixture, alternately

with the cocoa mixture. Divide and spread the batter ontothree prepared pans.
5. Bake in the oven for 25 to 30 minutes. Allow to cool for about 10 minutes. Turn upside down on wire rack to cool completely.
6. *To make Chocolate Icing:* Combine the chocolate and cream in a saucepan.Cook stirring constantly over low heat for 3 to 4 minutes or until smooth. Allow to cool for 10 minutes. Refrigerate until ready to use.
7. *To assemble the cake:*Cut the cake horizontally to make 3 even layers. Spread a thick layer of icing over one cake layer. Then, top with another layer of cake and spread more icing onto the cake. Repeat procedure for the last cake layer. Spread the remaining icing over the top and sides of the cake using a spatula.
8. Top with few berries.
9. Serve and enjoy.

Bittersweet Chocolate Cake Recipe

This decadent chocolate cake is great for dessert or snack.

Preparation Time: 15 minutes
Total Time: 60 minutes
Yield: 10 servings

Ingredients

2 cups white sugar
2 cups all-purpose flour
2 tsp. baking powder
2 tsp. baking powder

1 cup unsweetened cocoa powder
1 pinch salt
2/3 cup unsalted butter
2 cups boiling water
3 medium eggs, beaten
2 tsp. vanilla extract
Cooking oil spray

Bittersweet Chocolate Icing:
16 oz. bittersweet chocolate chips
1 ½ cup heavy cream

Method
1. Preheat oven to 350 F. Grease a 10-inch round pan with cooking oil spray.
2. Sift and mix together the sugar, all-purpose flour, baking powder, cocoa powder and salt in a large mixing bowl. Set aside.
3. Melt the butter in boiling water. Stir onto the flour mixture until just combined. Beat the eggs then stir in vanilla. Place the batter in a prepared pan.
4. Bake in the oven for 30 minutes or until a toothpick inserted into the

cake's center comes out clean. Allow to cool on wire rack.

5. *To make Chocolate Icing:* Put chocolate and cream in a saucepan over low heat. Cook, stirring constantly for 3 to 5 minutes or until smooth. Allow to cool for 10 minutes. Refrigerate until ready to use.

6. *To assemble the cake:* Trim the top to make the surface even. Split the cake in half horizontally to make two even layers. Invert top layer on a cake stand. Spread a thick layer of icing on top of the cake. Then, top with another layer of cake and spread more icing on top and sides of the cake using a spatula.

7. Serve and enjoy.

Cake Recipes

Delicious Chocolate Coffee Cake Recipe

This simple chocolate cake recipe gives youa moist, sweet and absolutely delicious dessert.

Preparation Time:15 minutes
Total Time:60 minutes
Yield:10 servings

Ingredients
1 ¼ cups all-purpose flour
1 cup brown sugar
1 tsp. baking soda
¾ cup unsweetened cocoa powder

1 tsp. salt
½ cup unsalted butter
1 tsp. vanilla extract
2medium eggs
2/3 cup strong brewed coffee, cooled
Cooking oil spray
Whipped cream, to serve

Method

1. Preheat oven to 350 F. Grease a 9 x 9-inchpan with oil spray.
2. Sift and mix together sugar, flour, baking soda, salt, and cocoa in a large mixing bowl. Set aside.
3. Using an electric mixer, cream the butter and sugar in a medium bowl until fluffy and pale in color.
4. Add the vanilla extract and egg.Beat until combined well. Add flour mixture, alternating with coffee. Mix until just combined.
5. Bake for 35 to 45 minutes or until a toothpick inserted at the center of the cake

comes out clean. Cool completely on wire rack.
6. Cut into 10 slices. Top with whipped cream.
7. Serve and enjoy.

Fabulous Chocolate Mocha Cake Recipe

The chocolate and coffee flavor blends perfectly in this great tasting cake recipe!

Preparation Time: 20 minutes
Total Time: 60 minutes
Yield: 12 servings

Ingredients

2 cups brown sugar
2 cups all-purpose flour
2/3 cup unsweetened cocoa powder
½ cup vegetable oil
2 large eggs

1 cup buttermilk
2 tsp. baking soda
2 tsp. baking powder
½ tsp. salt
3 Tbsp. instant coffee granules
1 cup hot water
Cooking oil spray
Whipped cream, to serve
Chocolate syrup, to serve

Semi-Sweet Chocolate Icing:
16 oz. semi-sweet chocolate chips
1 cup heavy cream
1 tsp. instant coffee granules

Method
1. Preheat oven to 350 F. Grease two 9-inch round cake pans with oil spray.
2. Mix together the sugar, flour, cocoa, oil, eggs, buttermilk, baking soda, baking powder, and salt in a large mixing bowl. Dissolve the instant coffee in hot water then place into the mixing bowl. Using an electric mixer, beat at medium speed for 2 minutes or until

smooth. Pour the mixture into the prepared pans.
3. Bake for 30 to 35 minutes or until a toothpick inserted at the center of the cake comes out clean. Cool in pans for 10 minutes. Turn the cake upside down onto wire racks to cool completely.
4. Meanwhile, melt the semi-sweet chocolate chips in a double broiler. Add cream and coffee.Cook for 1-2 minutes, stirring until combined well.
5. Cut the cake horizontally with serrated knife to make 2 even layers. Spread chocolate icing generously on the cake. Place the second cake layer and spread remaining icing on top and sides of the cake.
6. Serve with whipped cream and drizzle with some chocolate syrup.
7. Serve and enjoy.

Cake Recipes

Mom's Awesome Chocolate Cake Recipe

A classic chocolate cake recipe that you and your family will surely love!

Preparation Time: 20 minutes
Total Time: 60 minutes
Yield: 12 servings

Ingredients
2 cups white sugar
½ cup shortening
2 large eggs
1 cup whole milk
1¼ cup unsweetened cocoa powder

2 cups all-purpose flour
2 tsp. baking powder
2 tsp. baking soda
1 cup boiling water
2 tsp. vanilla extract
Cooking oil spray

Dark Chocolate Icing:
16 oz. dark chocolate, roughly chopped
1 cup heavy cream

Method

1. Preheat oven to 350 F. Grease a 10-inch round baking pan with oil spray.
2. Cream the shortening and sugar together until fluffy. Add the cocoa powder, flour, baking powder, baking soda, and vanilla extract.Pour the boiling water and mix until just combined. Transfer batter onto the prepared pans.
3. Bake for 30 to 35 minutes. Cool 10 minutes on the pan. Turn upside down and cool completely on a wire rack.
4. Meanwhile, combine the dark chocolate and cream in a double

broiler. Cook for 1-2 minutes, stirring until smooth. Refrigerate for a few minutes or until ready to use.
5. Cut the cake horizontally with serrated knife to make 3 even layers. Spread chocolate icing on each cake layer. Place one layer on top of each other and spread remaining icing on top and sides of the cake.
6. Serve and enjoy.

Rich Chocolate Lava Cake Recipe

This chocolate lava recipe is perfect for all chocolate lovers out there!

Preparation Time: 15 minutes
Total Time: 30 minutes
Yield: 12 servings

Ingredients

10 oz. semi-sweet chocolate chips
½ cup (1 stick)unsalted butter
½ tsp. vanilla extract
½ cup brown sugar
½ cupall-purpose flour

Cake Recipes

¼ tsp. salt
4 large eggs
Cooking oil spray
Flour, for dusting

Method

1. Preheat oven at 375 F. Grease muffin tin with oil spray. Dust with flour.
2. In a double boiler combine the chocolate chips, butter, and vanilla extract. Cook until melted and smooth.
3. In a large bowl combine sugar, cocoa powder, flour, and salt.
4. Place chocolate mixture in a large mixing bowl. With an electric mixer, add the eggs one at a time until each one is incorporated. Reduce speed on low, gradually add the dry ingredients until smooth.
5. Using a ladle put 4oz. batter onto each muffin tin. Bake for 10-12 minutes.
6. Cakeshould have crusty sides and gooey enters.

7. Serve and enjoy.

CAKES WITH FRUITS

Lemon And Ricotta Bars Recipe

Treat yourself with these delightful lemon cake bars with ricotta.

Preparation Time: 30 minutes
Total Time: 1 hours 30 minutes
Yield: 12 servings

Ingredients
1 ¾ cups graham crackers, crushed
½ cup butter, melted
8 oz. cream cheese
8 oz. ricotta cheese

½ cup caster sugar
2 Tbsp. all-purpose flour
3 medium eggs
½ cup all-purpose cream
1 Tbsp. lemon juice
1 Tbsp. lemon zest

Method
1. Preheat oven to 350 F.
2. Combine the crushed graham and butter in a mixing bowl. Mix well. Press half of the mixture onto the bottom of a 9x9-inch baking pan. Bake for 10 minutes in the oven. Cool in wire rack.
3. Using electric mixer, beat the cream cheese, ricotta, caster sugar, and flour until smooth. Add the eggs one at a time, cream, lemon juice, and zest. Mix until just combined.
4. Pour the cream cheese filling over the prepared crust. Top with remaining crust mixture.
5. Bake for one hour or until cooked through. Cool in wire rack. Chill for at least 4 hours or until ready to serve.

Cake Recipes

6. Cut into 12 bars.
7. Serve and enjoy.

Strawberry Mascarpone Cream Cake Recipe

This fabulous cake recipe with mascarpone cheese and strawberries makes a great dessert for any occasion. The fresh strawberry topping compliments well with the cake.

Preparation Time: 20 minutes
Total Time: 1 hour 45 minutes
Yield: 10 servings

Ingredients
1 ¾ cups shortbread cookies, crushed

½ cup butter, melted
2 Tbsp. cold water
1 Tbsp. gelatin powder
8 oz. cream cheese
8 oz. mascarpone cheese
½ cup condensed milk
½ cup sour cream
1 tsp. pure vanilla extract
Freshstrawberries, to serve

Method

1. In a large bowl, combine crushed cookies and butter. Mix well. Press onto the bottom and sides of a 9-inch spring form pan. Cover and chill until ready to use.
2. Combine 2 Tbsp. cold water and gelatine in a small bowl, mix until softened. Place the bowl in a pan of hot water and stir with a fork until dissolved. Allow to cool.
3. Using electric mixer, beat the cream cheese, mascarpone, condensed milk, and sour cream, until smooth. Add the prepared gelatine mixture. Beat briefly just to combine. Pour cream cheese filling over the prepared crust.

Chill for at least 4 hours or until ready to serve.
4. Top cheesecake with strawberries.
5. Serve and enjoy.

Cake Recipes

Special Strawberry Mousse Cake Recipe

If you are looking for a great tasting cake to serve your family and friends, this is the recipe for you!

Preparation Time: 20 minutes
Total Time: 50 minutes
Yield: 10 servings

Ingredients
4 eggwhites
¾ cup caster sugar
1 tsp. vanilla extract
¼ cup plain flour, sifted

1 tsp. lemon zest, finely grated
2 ½ cups all-purpose cream
6 oz. white chocolate, chopped
10 oz. fresh strawberries, plus extra to serve
1/3 cup strawberry jam
1/3 cup fresh strawberries, halved
1/3 cup slivered almonds, toasted
Icing sugar, to dust
Cooking oil spray
Fresh strawberries, to serve

Method

1. Preheat oven to 350 F. Grease and line the base of two 9-inch springform cake pans.
2. Using an electric mixer, whisk the eggwhites until soft peaks form. Slowly add the caster sugar. Beat until glossy and stiff. Stir in vanilla.
3. Combine the flour, almond meal and zest. Gradually fold into the egg white mixture. Divide batter into two pans and bake for about 15 minutes or until golden in color and tops are soft to the touch. Cool cakes in pans.

4. *To make the Mousse:* Bring 1 cup cream to a simmer over medium heat. Remove from heat, then add the white chocolate. Stir until chocolate has melted and smooth. Set aside to cool.
5. Combine the 2 tablespoons jam and fresh strawberries in a food processor. Allow the mixture to pass through a sieve, discard the solids. Fold onto the chocolate mixture.
6. Using an electric beater, whisk ½ cup cream until soft peaks are noted. Fold into the strawberry mixture using a metal spoon. Spread the mixture on one layer of cake. Top with another cake layer.Chill for at least 3 hours.
7. Whip 1 cup cream using electric beater until soft peaks appear, spread it over the top and sides of the cake. Sprinkle with almonds. Dust the cake with icing sugar and serve with berries.
8. Enjoy.

Mango Ricotta Cheesecake Recipe

This delightful mango cheesecake with ricotta is the perfect way to end a sumptuous meal.

Preparation Time: 30 minutes
Total Time: 30 minutes
Yield: 10 servings

Ingredients
1 ½ cups graham crackers, crushed
¼ cup butter, melted
¼ cup brown sugar

2 Tbsp. cold water
1 Tbsp. gelatin powder
2 (8oz.) cream cheese
½ cup caster sugar
1 tsp. pure vanilla extract
½ cup ricotta cheese
½ cup all-purpose cream
2 cups diced mangoes
Fresh mint, to serve

Method

1. In a large bowl, combine crushed graham, butter, and sugar. Mix well. Press onto the bottom of a 9-inch spring form pan. Cover and chill until ready to use.
2. Place cold water and gelatine in a small bowl, mix until softened. Put the bowl in a pan of hot water and stir with a fork until dissolved. Allow to cool.
3. Using electric mixer, beat the cream cheese, caster sugar, and vanilla extract until smooth. Gradually add the ricotta, cream, and prepared gelatine mixture. Beat briefly just to combine. Pour cream cheese filling over the

prepared crust. Chill for 4 hours or until ready to serve.
4. Top cheesecake with mangoes and fresh mint.
5. Serve and enjoy.

Angel Food Cake With Sweet Cherries Recipe

The cake is so fluffy and tastes so heavenly, it makes a great snack or dessert!

Preparation Time: 20 minutes
Total Time: 50 minutes
Yield: 8 servings

Ingredients

¼ tsp. salt
6 eggwhites
1 tsp. cream of tartar
1 tsp. pure vanilla extract
1 cup caster sugar
2/3 cup all-purpose flour, sifted

1 ½ cup vanilla frosting

Cherry Topping:
½ cup water
½ cup white sugar
¼ cup cherry brandy
1 lb. fresh cherries

Method

1. Preheat oven to 350 F. Line the base of a 10-inchround pan with non-stick baking paper.
2. Using an electric mixer, beat eggwhites, cream of tartar, and salt in a large mixing bowluntil soft peaks form. Add gradually the sugar (2 tablespoons at a time). Beating well after each addition until mixture becomes thick and glossy. Stir in vanilla extract. Fold in the flour until just combined.
3. Transfer batter onto the prepared pan and gently smoothen the surface.
4. Bake in preheated oven for 20 to 25 minutes or until firm to touch and golden. Turn the cake pan

upside down on a wire rack and allow the cake to cool totally.
5. *To prepare the Cherry topping:* Combine the water and sugar in a medium saucepan and bring to a boil over medium-high heat. Add the cherries and cherry brandy. Cook for 7-10 minutes. Remove from heat.
6. Cut the cake horizontally with serrated knife. Spread frosting on top of one cake layer. Place second layer on top and spread remaining frosting on top and at the sides of the cake.
7. Slice and serve the cake with prepared cherry topping.

Almond Cake With Orange And Polenta Recipe

This lovely cake recipe has a great blend of flavors from the almond, orange, and polenta.

Preparation Time: 20 minutes
Total Time: 1 hour 20 minutes
Yield: 8 servings

Ingredients

4 oz.unsalted butter
1 tsp.pure vanilla extract
¾ cup caster sugar
2 large eggs
1 cup almond meal

1 cup polenta
1 tsp. baking powder
2 large oranges, grated zest and juiced
Whipped cream, to serve
Orange slices, to serve
Cooking oil spray

Method
1. Preheat oven to 300 F. Grease a 9-inch round cake pan with oil spray. Line with baking paper on the base of the greased pan.
2. Using an electric mixer, cream the butter, sugar, and vanilla together in a large mixing bowl until fluffy and light in color. Add the eggs one at a time, beating well after each addition.
3. Addthe almond meal, polenta, baking powder, orange zest, and juice.Stir until well combined. Pour batter onto the prepared pan.
4. Bake for 55 to 60 minutes or until a toothpick inserted into the cake comes out clean. Cool for about 10 minutes on the pan. Place onto a wire rack to cool.

5. Serve with orange slices and whipped cream on top.
6. Enjoy.

Coconut Orange Cake Recipe

The ingredients in this recipe is perfectly combined to produce a yummy cake.

Preparation Time: 20 minutes
Total Time: 60 minutes
Yield: 10 servings

Ingredients

3 medium oranges
1 ½ cups caster sugar
1 cup unsalted butter, softened
5 large eggs, separated
1 ½ cups desiccated coconut
1 ½ cups self-raising flour, sifted
1 ½ cups fresh, white breadcrumbs

Cooking oil spray

Syrup:
½ cup fresh orange juice
1 Tbsp. orange zest, finely grated
1 vanilla bean
1 ½ cups white sugar

Method
1. Preheat oven to 350 F. Grease a 10-inchbaking pan with oil spray. Line the base with a non-stick baking paper.
2. Get zest from 1 orange. Using juice extractor, squeeze all oranges. Reserve juice.
3. In a large mixing bowl, cream butter and sugar using an electric mixer until creamy and light in color. Add the eggyolks, one at a time. Beating well between additions. Add orange rind, coconut and 1 cup orange juice. Mix on low speed until well combined.
4. Add the flour and breadcrumbs tothe orange-coconut mixture. Stir until just combined.

5. Beat eggwhites using clean beaters until soft peaks appear. Gentlyfold into the cake batter. Transfer the mixture onto the prepared pan. Bake for about 30 to 35 minutes until a toothpick inserted at the center of the cake comes out clean. Allow to cool completely onthe pan.
6. *To make the syrup:*Combine orange juice, zest, vanilla bean, and sugar in a sauce pan over medium heat. Cook, stir frequently for 10 minutes or until syrup becomes slightly thick.
7. Slice cake and serve with syrup.
8. Enjoy.

Luscious Lemon Yogurt Cake Recipe

A perfect way to treat yourself on weekends. This cake hasgreat blend of flavors from the lemon and yogurt.

Preparation Time: 20 minutes
Total Time: 1 hour 45 minutes
Yield: 6-8 servings

Ingredients

1 medium lemon
½ cupunsalted butter
½ cup caster sugar

2 large eggs
6 oz. Greek yogurt
1 cup self-raising flour, sifted
Cooking oil spray
Icing sugar, for dusting

Method

1. Preheat oven to 350 F. Grease a 9x9-inch cake pan with oil spray.
2. Grate finely the lemon rind and juice the fruit using a juice extractor. Measure ¼ cup of lemon juice.
3. In a large mixing bowl, cream butter and sugar using electric beaters until fluffy and light in color.
4. Add the eggs one at a time. Beating well after each addition.
5. Add the yogurt, rind and juice. Mix until just combined.
6. Gently fold the flour using a wooden spoon until combined. Pour the mixture into the prepared pan and smooth the surface using the spoon. Bake for 20 to 25 minutes or until a toothpick inserted at the center of the cake

comes out clean. Remove from oven. Place the cake on a wire rack.
7. Dust cake with icing sugar and cut into small squares.
8. Serve and enjoy.

Easy Semolina And Lemon Cake Recipe

This lemon cake was made different with the inclusion of semolina.

Preparation Time: 20 minutes
Total Time: 1 hour 20 minutes
Yield: 10 servings

Ingredients
½ cup and 2 Tbsp. unsalted butter, softened
1 Tbsp. lemon zest, finely grated
1 cup caster sugar
2 large eggs

2/3 cup semolina
1 ½ cup self-raising flour, sifted
½ cup whole milk
Cooking oil spray

Method
1. Preheat oven to 350 F. Grease a 9-inch round cake pan. Line the side and base with non-stick baking paper.
2. Cream butter and sugar using an electric mixer on high speed until light in color. Add eggs one at a time, beating well after each addition. Stir in lemon zest, semolina, flour, and milk.
3. Pour the mixture into prepared pan. Bake for 45 to 50 minutes or until a toothpick inserted into the center comes out clean. Cool in wire rack.
4. Serve and enjoy.

Apple Almond Cake Recipe

If you love the taste of apple and almonds in your cake, then this is the perfect recipe for you!

Preparation Time: 20 minutes
Total Time: 1 hour 45 minutes
Yield: 12 servings

Ingredients
½ cup unsalted butter
1 tsp.pure vanilla extract
½ cup caster sugar
3medium eggs
4 oz.dry roasted almonds, ground

6oz. self-raising flour, sifted
½ cup whole milk
2 medium apples, peeled, cored and thinly sliced
Cooking oil spray
Icing sugar, for dusting

Method

1. Preheat oven to 350 F. Grease a 9x9-inch cake pan with oil spray. Line the base and sides with non-stick baking paper.
2. Using an electric mixer, creambutter with caster sugar and vanilla in a large mixing bowl until fluffy and light in color.
3. Add eggs one at a time, beating well after each addition.
4. Stir in ground almonds. Gradually add the flour alternately with milk.Mix until combined.
5. Arrange the slices of apple on base of the prepared pan. Pour the batter onto the pan and smooth the surface using a spatula.
6. Bake for 30 to 35 minutes or until a toothpick inserted into the center of the cake comes out clean.

Cake Recipes

Remove from heat. Allow to cool in wire rack.
7. Dust cake with icing sugar. Cut into 12 slices.
8. Serve and enjoy.

Mini Ring Cake With Ricotta And Raspberry Recipe

Let your kids enjoy in making these yummy little cakes with raspberries.

Preparation Time: 20 minutes
Total Time: 40 minutes
Yield: 6 servings

Ingredients

1 ½ cups all-purpose flour
1 tsp. baking powder
¼ tsp. salt
¾ cup unsalted butter

1 cup sugar
3 large eggs, lightly beaten
1 tsp. pure vanilla extract
6 oz. ricotta cheese
1 cup fresh raspberries
¼ cup pistachio nuts, coarsely chopped

Method

1. Place rack at the lower third of an oven and preheat to 325 F. Generously grease and flour a six mini ring pan or mini Bundt pan.
2. Combine and sift together the flour, baking powder and salt. Set aside.
3. Using an electric mixer, beat the butter on medium speed until creamy and smooth, about 1-2 minutes. Add the sugar and beat until fluffy and light in color.
4. Add the eggs gradually, beating well after each addition. Stir in the vanilla extract. Reduce the speed to low. Add the flour mixture in three additions, mixinguntil just combined.Pour the batter into the prepared pan and spread evenly with spatula.

5. Bake until a toothpick inserted near the center of a cake comes out clean, about 20-25 minutes. Transfer the pan to a wire rack and let the cakes cool upside down in the pan for 10 minutes, then gently remove the cake from the pan. Cool completely on the wire rack.
6. Serve the mini cakes with a dollop of ricotta cheese and raspberries on top. Sprinkle with pistachios.
7. Enjoy.

Sweet Apple Cake With Walnuts Recipe

Give in to your sweet cravings with these delightful cake with apples and walnuts.

Preparation Time: 20 minutes
Total Time: 60 minutes
Yield: 8 servings

Ingredients

2 medium apples, peeled, cored, and thinly sliced
1 ¼ cup all-purpose flour
1 tsp. baking soda
1 tsp. cinnamon, ground

1 cup brown sugar
½ cup butter, melted
1 medium egg, beaten
1 tsp. allspice
4 oz. walnuts
Cooking oil spray

Method

1. Preheat oven to 350 F. Grease a 9-inch spring form pan with oil spray and line with baking paper.
2. Combine the apple slices with flour, baking soda, cinnamon, brown sugar, allspice, and walnuts in a large mixing bowl. Stir in the egg and melted butter. Mix until combined.
3. Pour the mixture into a prepared pan and bake for 50-60 minutes or until cake is tested done.
4. Let the cake stand in pan for 10 minutes. Place in wire rack to cool.
5. Serve and enjoy.

COFFEE CAKES

Simple Coffee Cake Recipe

This simple and easy to make coffee cake is perfect for morning or afternoon snack!

Preparation Time: 15 minutes
Total Time: 45 minutes
Yield: 8 servings

Ingredients
2/3 cup butter
2/3 cup brown sugar
3 medium eggs

¾ cup self-raising flour
½ tsp. baking powder
2Tbsp.instant coffee powder
2Tbsp. hot water

Method

1. Preheat oven to 300 F. Grease a 9-inch Bundt pan with oil spray.
2. Using an electric mixer, cream the butter and sugar to a large mixing bowl. Whisk until mixture turns fluffy and light in color.
3. Gradually add the eggs, beating well after each addition.
4. Stir in the flour and baking powder gently until just combined.
5. Dissolve the coffee in boiling water. Add to the mixture.Pour the batter in the prepared pan. Bake for about 35 minutes. Turn onto a large plate to cool completely.
6. Dust the cake with icing sugar. Cut into 8 slices.
7. Serve and enjoy.

Streusel Coffee Cinnamon Cake With Pecans Recipe

This great tasting coffee cake recipe is a must try!

Preparation Time: 25 minutes
Total Time: 1 hour and 25 minutes
Yield: 10-12 servings

Ingredients
For the Streusel topping and center:
1 ¾ cup all-purpose flour
1 cup brown sugar
1 ½ tsp. cinnamon, ground
½ tsp. salt

1 ½ cup dry roasted pecans

For the cake:
½ cup unsalted butter
2 cups all-purpose flour
1 ¼ tsp. baking powder
½ tsp. baking soda
½ tsp. salt
1 cup brown sugar
2 large eggs
1 ½ tsp.pure vanilla extract
1 cup sour cream
Cooking oil spray

For the glaze:
1 cup caster sugar
2 Tbsp. whole milk

Method
1. Preheat oven to 350 degrees F. Grease a 10-inch pan with oil spray.
2. *To make the Topping:* Combine the flour, ¾ cup brown sugar, 1 teaspoon cinnamon powder, and salt. Using a pastry cutter, cut in the butter. Add half of the pecans. Put in the fridge until ready to use.

3. *To make the Streusel center:* Combine the remaining sugar, cinnamon andpecans.
4. *To make the cake:* Sift baking soda, flour, baking powder and ½ teaspoon salt into a large mixing bowl.Using an electric mixer on medium speed, beat butter and granulated sugar in a separate bowl for 2 minutes or until fluffy and light in color. Beat in eggs one at a time then add in the vanilla extract. Add the flour mixture in 3 additions, alternating with sour cream (starting and ending with flour). Mix until just combined.
5. Pour half the batter into the prepared pan. Sprinkle streusel center mixture evenly. Pour remaining batter and sprinkle streusel topping mixture. Bake in prepared pan for 55 minutes or until golden brown or a toothpick inserted at the center of the cake comes out clean. Transfer pan to a wire rack, to cool completely.
6. *To make the Glaze:* Combine milk and caster sugar. Drizzle over cake.

Let sit for 5-7 minutes before serving. Cut cake into 10 slices.
7. Serve and enjoy.

Sour Cream Coffee Cake With Walnuts Recipe

This coffee cake recipe is filling and very delicious!

Preparation Time: 20 minutes
Total Time: 1 hour 40 minutes
Yield: 10 servings

Ingredients
¾ cup unsalted butter, softened
1 ½ cup brown sugar
4 large eggs
1 ¼ cup sour cream

1 ½ tsp. pure vanilla extract
2 ½ cup self-raising cake flour
½ tsp. baking soda
½ tsp. salt
Cooking oil spray

For the Streusel:
¼ cup light brown sugar
1 ½ tsp. cinnamon, ground
½ cup all-purpose flour
3 Tbsp. cold unsalted butter, cut into pieces
¼ tsp. salt
¾ cup walnuts, chopped

For the Honey Glaze:
½ cup caster sugar
2 Tbsp. pure honey

Method

1. Preheat oven to 350 degrees F. Grease and flour a 10-inch round cake pan.
2. Using an electric mixer, cream the butter and sugar in a large mixing bowl for 3-4 minutes or until light and fluffy. Gradually add eggs, beating well after each addition.

Add the sour cream and vanilla extract. Sift together the flour, baking soda, baking powder and salt in a separate mixing bowl. Fold the flour mixture onto the egg mixture until combined well.
3. *For the Streusel:* combine the brown sugar, cinnamon, flour, butter and salt in a large mixing bowl and rub with your fingers until it forms a crumble. Add the walnuts.
4. Pour half the batter into the pan. Spread it out with a spatula. Sprinkle with ¾ cup streusel. Add the remaining batter in the pan. Spread it out and sprinkle with the rest of the streusel on top.
5. Bake for 50 to 60 minutes or until a toothpick inserted into the cake comes out clean.
6. Let cool on a wire rack. Transfer the cake on a large plate with the streusel side up.
7. In a small bowl, mix togethercaster sugar and honey. Then add a few drops of water to make the glaze a bit runny. Drizzle over the cake.

8. Serve and enjoy.

◆◆◆◆◆◆◆◆◆

Apple Coffee Caramel Cake Recipe

Take your regular snacks to new heights by following this delicious coffee cake recipe!

Preparation Time: 25 minutes
Total Time: 1 hour and 25 minutes
Yield: 10 servings

Ingredients
2 Tbsp. butter
3 cups peeled, cored and sliced apples

Streusel Topping:
½ cup butter, softened

1 cup brown sugar
2 large eggs

Apple Coffee Cake:
2 tsp. baking powder
2 cups all-purpose flour
½ tsp. salt
2/3 cup whole milk
1 ½ tsp.pure vanilla extract

For the glaze:
1 cup caster sugar
2 Tbsp. whole milk

Method

1. Preheat oven to 350 degrees F. Grease and flour 9-inch spring form pan.
2. Melt 2 tablespoons butter over medium high heat in a large saucepan. Add apples. Cook for 6 minutes or until the apples are soft. Remove from heat. Allow to cool. Set aside.
3. *To prepare Streusel topping and Caramel sauce*: Cream butter using an electronic mixer at medium speed until light in color. Add

sugar, gradually. Add eggs one at a time, beat until well blended after each addition.
4. *To make the Glaze:* In a small bowl, combine caster sugar and milk. Set aside.
5. Mix together baking powder, flour and salt. Add to butter mixture alternately with flour mixture. Beat at low speed until blended after each addition. Stir in vanilla. Spoon the batter into a prepared pan. Top with sliced apples. Drizzle with Caramel sauce. Sprinkle with streusel topping.
6. Cover loosely with foil and bake for 45 minutes or until a cake tester comes out clean. Remove foil and coolon a wire rack. Transfer in a large plate. Drizzle with glaze.
7. Serve and enjoy.

Crunchy Almond Cherry Coffee Cake Recipe

If you are looking for something that you can pair with your coffee for breakfast or snack time, this is the recipe for you!

Preparation Time: 25 minutes
Total Time: 55 minutes
Yield: 10 servings

Ingredients

½ cup Greek yogurt
3 Tbsp. vegetable oil
½ cup whole milk

1 large egg
2 cups all-purpose flour + 1 tablespoon, divided
½ cup brown sugar + 1 tablespoon, divided
2 tsp. baking powder
1 tsp. baking soda
½ tsp. salt
1 ½ cup fresh cherries, pitted
2 Tbsp. sliced almonds
1 tsp. cinnamon, ground

Method

1. Preheat oven to 400 degrees F. Grease and flour a 9-inch spring form pan.
2. Whisk together the yogurt, vegetable oil, milk and egg in a large bowl.
3. Sift together flour, sugar and baking powder in a medium bowl. Stir egg mixture into flour mixture until just combined.
4. Toss 1 ¼ cup cherries in 1 tablespoon flour. Fold into batter. Pour the batter in the prepared pan. Top with remaining cherries.

5. Stir together remaining 2 tablespoons sugar, cinnamon and sliced almonds. Sprinkle over batter.
6. Bake for 25 to 30 minutes until a toothpick inserted at the center of the cake comes out clean. Cool on wire rack.
7. Serve and enjoy.

Grandma's Delicious Coffee Cake With Blueberries Recipe

Blueberries and walnuts adds a nice touch to this awesome coffee cake.

Preparation Time: 20 minutes
Total Time: 50 minutes
Yield: 12 servings

Ingredients

¾ cup white sugar
2 cups all- purpose flour
2 tsp. baking powder
½ tsp. salt
½ cup butter

1 large egg
¾ cup whole milk
1 ½ tsp. pure vanilla extract
1 ½ cup blueberries

For Streusel topping:
2/3 cup brown sugar
¼ cup all-purpose flour
1 tsp. cinnamon, ground
½ cup walnuts
¼ cup butter

Method

1. Preheat oven to 350 F. Grease and flour a 10-inch round baking pan.
2. *To make the streusel topping:* Combine the sugar, flour, and cinnamon in a medium bowl. Cut in butter until mixture resembles coarse crumbs. Add the walnuts. Set aside.
3. Combine sugar, flour, baking powder, and salt in a large bowl. Cut in butter until mixture resembles crumbs. Crack an egg into a measuring cup and then add milk to make 1 cup. Stir in vanilla extract. Pour into the crumb

mixture and mix until just combined.Fold blueberries onto the batter. Spoon mixture and spread into prepared pan. Sprinkle top with streusel topping.
4. Bake for 25 to 30 minutes or until toothpick inserted at the center of the cake comes out clean. Cool completely on wire rack.
5. Serve and enjoy.

Cinnamon-Spiced Butter Cake Recipe

This is a simple yet delicious cake recipe, it is best served with a cup of coffee.

Preparation Time: 15 minutes
Total Time: 30 minutes
Yield: 6 servings

Ingredients

1 cup all-purpose flour, sifted
2 tsp. baking powder
1 tsp. baking soda
½ tsp. cinnamon, ground

½ cup whole milk
½ cup brown sugar
½ tsp. salt
2/3 cup butter, melted
1 large egg
Cooking oil spray
Icing sugar, to serve

Method
1. Preheat oven to 350 F. Grease and flour a 6-cup Bundt cake pan.
2. Combine all ingredients in a large bowl.Pour batter into the prepared pan.
3. Bake for 15 to 20 minutes or until a toothpick inserted at the center of the cake comes out clean.Cool on a wire rack. Transfer on a large plate and dust cake with icing sugar.
4. Serve and enjoy.

Easy Buttermilk Coffee Cake Recipe

This easy coffee cake recipe is great for breakfast, snack or dessert. Your friends and family will surely enjoyevery bite!

Preparation Time: 20 minutes
Total Time: 50 minutes
Yield: 12 servings

Ingredients

1 ½ cup white sugar
2 ¼ cup all-purpose flour
¾ tsp. baking soda
1 ½ tsp. baking powder

½ cup butter, softened
1 cup buttermilk
½ tsp.pure vanilla extract
2 large eggs

Method

1. Preheat oven to 350 F. Grease and flour a 9x13-inch pan.
2. Combine sugar, flour, baking soda, and baking powder in a large bowl. Cut butter into the flour mixture until mixture resembles crumbs. Gently stir in buttermilk, vanilla extract, and eggs into batter until just combined. Pour batter into prepared baking pan.
3. Bake for 35 minutes or until a toothpick inserted at the center of the cake comes out clean. Remove from heat.Cool on wire rack.
4. Serve and enjoy.

TEA CAKES

Golden Butter Cake Recipe

A tasty and easy butter cake that is great for an afternoon tea.

Preparation Time: 20 minutes
Total Time: 1 hours 20 minutes
Yield: 10 servings

Ingredients

1 cup white sugar
¾ cup unsalted butter, softened
2 large eggs
1 ½ tsp. pure vanilla extract
2 cups all-purpose flour

Cake Recipes

2 tsp. baking powder
½ tsp. salt
¾ cup whole milk
Icing sugar, to serve

Method

1. Preheat oven to 350 F. Grease and flour a 9x5x3-inch loaf pan.
2. Using an electric mixer, cream butter and sugar in a large bowl until fluffy and light in color. Add eggs one at a time, beating until combined. Stir in the vanilla extract. Combine the baking powder, flour and salt in a separate bowl. Stir into the batter alternately with milk. Pour the batter evenly into the prepared pan.
3. Bake for 30 to 35 minutes until a toothpick inserted at the center of the cake comes out clean. Cool in pan on wire rack. Transfer in a large plate and dust with icing sugar.
4. Serve and enjoy.

Buttermilk Sultana Tea Cake Recipe

This delectable teacake recipe with buttermilkand sultanasis really good for a quick breakfast or snack.

Preparation Time: 20 minutes
Total Time: 1 hour 45 minutes
Yield: 10 servings

Ingredients

1 ½ cups all-purpose flour
2 Tbsp. baking powder
1 tsp. baking soda
½ tsp. salt
1 large egg
½ cup buttermilk

1 cup brown sugar
¼ cup vegetable oil
1 tsp.pure vanilla extract
1 cup sultana raisins
½ cup dry roasted cashews, coarsely chopped

Method

1. Preheat oven to 350 degrees F. Grease and flour a 9-inch Bundt pan.
2. Combine flour, baking powder, baking soda, and salt in a small bowl. In a large bowl, whisk together egg, buttermilk, brown sugar, vanilla extract, and oil until combined well. Gradually, stir in the flour mixture, sultanas, and cashews until just combined. Pour mixture onto the prepared pan.
3. Bake in the oven for 1 hour or until a toothpick inserted at the center of the cake comes out clean. Cool in wire rack. Remove from pan. Transfer in a large plate.
4. Serve and enjoy.

Sweet And Simple Lemon Tea Cake Recipe

This is the perfect cake to pair with your tea during snack time.

Preparation Time: 20 minutes
Total Time: 1 hour 15 minutes
Yield: 10 servings

Ingredients

1 cup self-raising flour
1 1/3 cups all-purpose flour
1 1/3 cups powdered sugar
3 large eggs
6 oz. butter, melted and cooled
1 Tbsp. lemon rind, finely grated

½ cup whole milk
1/3 cupfresh lemon juice
Cooking oil spray

Method
1. Preheat oven to350 F. Grease and flour a 9-inch Bundt pan.
2. In a large mixing bowl, sift together self-raising flour, all-purpose flour, and sugar. Make a well in the center.
3. In a separate mixing bowl, whisk together the eggs, butter, lemon rind, milk and 1/3 cup lemon juice.
4. Add the lemon mixture into the flour mixture. Stir until just combined. Pour into the prepared pan and smoothen the surface with spatula. Bake for 40 to 45 minutes or until a toothpick inserted into the center of the cake comes out clean. Place in wire rack and allow to cool.
5. Transfer the cake on a serving platter.
6. Serve and enjoy.

Dates And Cinnamon Tea Cake Recipe

This tea cake recipe is a sure crowd-pleaser, you can enjoy it anytime of the day.

Preparation Time: 20 minutes
Total Time: 1 hour 20 minutes
Yield: 8 servings

Ingredients

6 oz. butter, cubed
¾ cup brown sugar
1 tsp. pure vanilla extract
2 large eggs

1 ¼ cups self-raising flour
½ cup sour cream
1 tsp. cinnamon, ground
½ cup dried dates, coarsely chopped

Method

1. Preheat oven to 350 F. Grease and line a 9x5x3-inch loaf pan with baking paper.
2. Using an electric mixer cream butter, sugar, and vanilla together until smooth and fluffy. Add eggs one at a time, beating well after each addition of egg.
3. Sift cinnamon and flour together. Fold the flour and dates into the egg mixture alternately with sour cream. Pour into the prepared pan and smoothen the surface using a spatula. Bake for 1 hour or until toothpick inserted at the center of the cake comes out clean.
4. Cool in pan for 10-15 minutes. Gently, transfer onto a serving plate.
5. Serve and enjoy.

Supreme Carrot And Cinnamon Cake Recipe

This sweet and mildly spiced carrot cake is great for dessert or snack.

Preparation Time: 20 minutes
Total Time: 60 minutes
Yield: 12 servings

Ingredients

1 cup self-raising flour
½ cup whole meal flour
2 tsp. cinnamon, ground
¾ cup brown sugar
½ cup whole milk
¼ cup vegetable oil

2 large eggs, lightly beaten
2 large carrots, finely grated
Cooking oil spray
Icing sugar, for dusting

Method

1. Preheat oven to 350 F. Grease and line a 8x8-inch cake pan with baking paper.
2. Sift together cinnamon and flour in a medium bowl. Stir in the sugar.
3. Whisk the oil, milk and eggs together in a separate mixing bowl. Slowly add to flour mixture and use a wooden spoon to mix until smooth.
4. Fold carrots into batter until combined well. Pour in prepared pan. Bake for 45 minutes or until a toothpick inserted at the center of the cake comes out clean. Cool for 5-10 minutes on the pan and transfer onto a wire rack to cool.
5. Cut cake into squares. Dust with icing sugar.
6. Serve and enjoy.

Carrot Walnut Cake With Cream Cheese Frosting Recipe

Enjoy a hot cup of tea and a slice of this awesome carrot cake!

Preparation Time: 20 minutes
Total Time: 1 hour 45 minutes
Yield: 10 servings

Ingredients
1 tsp. allspice
1 tsp. cinnamon, ground
2 cups self-raising flour
1 cup black walnuts, chopped

2 cups grated carrots
1 cup brown sugar
3 large eggs, lightly beaten
1 cup vegetable oil

For Cream Cheese Frosting:
1 Tbsp. lemon rind, finely grated
8 oz. cream cheese, softened
1 ½ cups icing sugar mixture

Method
1. Preheat oven to 350 F. Grease and line a 10-inch cake pan using non-stick baking paper.
2. Sift together allspice, cinnamon and flour in a large mixing bowl. Add walnuts, carrots, sugar, eggs, and oil. Stir to combine well. Pour and spread into prepared pan.
3. Bake for 1 hour and 15 minutes or until a toothpick inserted at the center of the cake comes out clean. Allow to cool in pan for 10 minutes. Transfer onto a wire rack to cool completely.
4. *To make Cream Cheese frosting:* Beat cream cheese and lemon rind

using an electric mixer. Add sugar gradually and beat until smooth.
5. Cut the cake in half using a serrated knife to make 2 layers. Spread a thick layer of cream cheese frosting. Top with the second cake layer and spread the remaining frosting on top and at the sides of the cake.
6. Serve and enjoy.

Perfect Carrot And Pineapple Cake Recipe

The flavor of pineapple combines perfectly in this delicious carrot cake recipe.

Preparation Time: 20 minutes
Total Time: 1 hour 20 minutes
Yield: 10 servings

Ingredients
2 cups all-purpose flour
1 tsp. baking powder
2 tsp. baking soda
2 tsp. cinnamon, ground
1 tsp. salt

1 cup vegetable oil
1 ¾ cup white sugar
3 large eggs
1 tsp. pure vanilla extract
1 cup flaked coconut
1 cup chopped walnuts
8 oz. canned pineapple, crushed and drained
2 cups carrots, finely grated
Cooking oil spray

For the Cream Cheese Frosting:
8 oz. cream cheese
¼ cup butter, softened
2 cups caster sugar

Method
1. Preheat oven to 350 degrees F. Grease and flour a 10-inch round baking pan.
2. In a large mixing bowl, mix together the flour, baking powder, baking soda, cinnamon and salt. Make a well in the center. Add oil, sugar, eggs and vanilla extract. Mix the ingredients using a wooden spoon until smooth. Stir in the

coconut, walnuts, pineapple, and carrots until combined well.
3. Spread the batter in a 10-inch round baking pan. Bake for 45 minutes. Cool the cake in pan for 10 minutes. Transfer onto a wire rack to cool completely.
4. *To make the frosting:*Beat cream cheese and butter until smooth. Gradually add the caster sugar and continue beating until creamy.
5. Cut the cake in half using a serrated knife to make 2 layers. Spread a thick layer of cream cheese frosting. Top with the second cake layer and spread the remaining frosting on top and at the sides of the cake.
6. Serve and enjoy.

Easy Banana Walnut And Yogurt Cake Recipe

This cake recipe with banana, walnuts, and yogurt is so easy to make and very delicious.

Preparation Time: 15 minutes
Total Time: 1 hour 15 minutes
Yield: 10 servings

Ingredients
1 cup brown sugar
1 tsp. pure vanilla extract
6 oz. butter
3 large eggs

3 cups self-raising flour
1 tsp. baking soda
1 ½ cups mashed, over ripe banana
1 cup Greek yogurt

For the Icing:
8 oz. cream cheese
¼ cup icing sugar
½ cup Greek yogurt

Method
1. Preheat oven to 350 F. Grease a 9x5x3-inch loaf pan. Line with baking paper the base and sides of the cake pan.
2. Beat sugar, vanilla and butter using an electric mixer until fluffy and light in color. Add eggs one at a time, beating well until blended. Stir in sifted flour, baking soda, banana, and yogurt untiljust combined. Pour the mixture into the prepared greased pan andsmoothen the top with a spatula.
3. Bake for 1 hour or until a cake tester inserted at the center of the cake comes out clean. Cool in pan

for 10 minutes. Transfer cake onto a wire rack to cool completely.
4. To make an Icing:Beat cream cheese and sugar using an electric mixer until light. Add in yogurt until well combined. Spread the icing on top of the cake.
5. Serve and enjoy.

Banana Bundt Cake With Buttermilk Recipe

This scrumptious cake recipe is perfect during tea time.

Preparation Time: 20 minutes
Total Time: 1 hour 20 minutes
Yield: 10 servings

Ingredients
4 oz. butter,softened
1 ¼ cup over-ripe banana, mashed
1 ½ cup brown sugar
1 tsp.pure vanilla extract
½ cup buttermilk
1 ½ cup self-raising flour

½ tsp. baking soda
Icing sugar, for dusting

Method

1. Preheat oven to 350 F. Grease a 10-inch Bundt cake pan with oil spray.
2. Combine the banana, sugar, butter, vanilla and eggs in a food processor bowl. Process for 2 minutes or until well combined. Add the buttermilk, flour, and baking soda. Process until just combined. Pour the mixture onto the prepared pan.
3. Bake for 1 hour or until a cake tester inserted at the center of the cake comes out clean. Cool in pan for 10 minutes. Transfer cake onto a wire rack to cool completely.
4. Place the cake on a large pate. Dust with icing sugar.
5. Serve and Enjoy.

CHIFFON CAKES

Homemade Orange Chiffon Cake Recipe

Enjoy a little treat with your morning or afternoon tea, and thisorange chiffon cake does the job perfectly.

Preparation Time: 20 minutes
Total Time: 1 hour 20 minutes
Yield: 10 servings

Ingredients
2 ¼ cup flour
1 cup powdered sugar

2 tsp. baking powder
1 tsp. salt
8 large eggs, separated plus 1 white, at room temperature
½ cup vegetable oil
3 Tbsp. orange zest, finely grated
1 tsp. pure vanilla extract
1 tsp. cream of tartar

Method

1. Preheat oven to 325 F.
2. Sift flour, sugar, baking powder, and salt in a large mixing bowl.
3. Whisk together the oil, yolks, zest and vanilla extract in a separate bowl. Gradually add oil mixture into the flour mixture.
4. Using an electric mixer, beat eggwhites until frothy. Add cream of tartar, continue beating until firm. Gradually addthe sugar until stiff peaks form. Fold gently the egg white mixture onto the flour mixture.
5. Bake in an ungreased 10-inch spring form pan for 1 hour and 10 minutes until a toothpick inserted into the center of the cake comes

out clean. Place on a wire rack to cool. Carefully transfer to a large plate.
6. Serve and enjoy.

Zesty Orange Lemon Chiffon Cake Recipe

Got some orange and lemon? Here is the perfect recipe to use them up! This cake is soft and flavorful. The glaze made it even better.

Preparation Time: 20 minutes
Total Time: 1 hour 20 minutes
Yield: 10 servings

Ingredients

1 ½ cup powdered sugar
2 ½ cups sifted cake flour
1 Tbsp. baking powder

1 tsp. salt
5 large eggs, separated
½ cup vegetable oil
2/3 cup fresh orange juice
2 Tbsp. fresh lemon juice
2Tbsp. lemon zest, finely grated
½ tsp. cream of tartar

Orange Glaze:
½ cup fresh orange juice
1 pound confectioner's sugar, sifted

Method
1. Preheat oven to 325 F.
2. Sift ¾ cup sugar, cake flour, baking powder, and salt.
3. Whisk together the yolks, oil, juices, and zest in a separate bowl. Gradually stir in oil mixture into the flour mixture.
4. Beat eggwhites until frothy. Add cream of tartar then beat until firm. Add remaining ¾ cup sugar, 1 tablespoon at a time, until stiff peaks form. Fold gently the egg white mixture into the flour mixture. Pour batter in ungreased 10-inch spring form pan and bake

for 1 hour or until a toothpick inserted at the center of the cake comes out clean. Place on a wire rack to cool. Carefully transfer to a serving platter.
5. *To make Glaze:* In a small bowl, stir orange juice and sugar until dissolved. Drizzle over top of cake.
6. Serve and enjoy.

Cake Recipes

Classic Chiffon Cake Recipe

This cake recipe is great for your kid's birthday party. You can decorate it with any fruit you like and some whipped cream.

Preparation Time: 20 minutes
Total Time: 1 hour 30 minutes
Yield: 10 servings

Ingredients
2 cups cake flour, sifted
1 Tbsp. baking powder
1 ½ cup white sugar
1 tsp. salt
7 egg yolks

¾ cup cold water
2 tsp.pure vanilla extract
½ cup vegetable oil
1 tsp. lemon extract
7 egg whites
1 tsp. cream of tartar
½ cup vegetable oil
Whipped cream, to serve
Fruit slices, to serve

Method

1. Preheat oven to 325 F. Line a 9x13-inch pan with non-stick baking paper.
2. Combine cake flour, baking powder, white sugar, and salt in a large mixing bowl. Make a well in the center. Place the egg yolks, water, vanilla extract, oil and lemon extracton the well. Stir until just combined. Set aside.
3. Beat egg whites and cream of tartar in a separate mixing bowl until stiff.
4. Fold gently the egg white mixture onto the flour mixture with spatula. Pour the batter into the prepared pan.

Cake Recipes

5. Bake for 55 minutes. Adjust heat to 350 F. Bake further 10 minutes or until tested done. Transfer cake onto a wire rack tocool completely. Remove baking paper.
6. Top with fruit slices and whipped cream.
7. Serve and enjoy.

Special Mocha Chiffon Cake With Cashews Recipe

Here is a delicious treat for all cake lovers out there!

Preparation Time: 20 minutes
Total Time: 1 hour 20 minutes
Yield: 10 servings

Ingredients

½ cup powdered cocoa
1 Tbsp. instant coffee powder
¾ cup boiling water
1 ¾ cup cake flour, sifted
1 ½ tsp. baking soda
1 ¾ cup white sugar

½ tsp. salt
8 large eggs, separated
½ cup vegetable oil
2 tsp. vanilla extract
½ tsp. cream of tartar
¼ cup honey
1 cup dry roasted cashew nuts

For MochaButtercream Icing:
¾ cup butter, softened
2 ½ cup caster sugar
1 Tbsp. powdered cocoa
¾ cup whipping cream
2 Tbsp. coffee liqueur

Method
1. Preheat oven at 325 F.
2. Stir together cocoa, instant coffee granules and boiling water until well blended. Set aside and allow to cool.
3. Combine flour, baking soda, sugar and salt in a large mixing bowl. Add egg yolks, oil, vanilla, and cocoa mixture.Stir until smooth.
4. Beat egg whites and cream of tartar at high speed with an electric mixer until foamy. Fold the

egg white mixture into the flour mixture. Divide equally the batter into three greased and lined 9-inch round cake pans.

5. Bake 2 layers at a time, for 20 minutes or until a toothpick inserted ate the center of the cake comes out clean. Cool layers in pans or on wire racks for 10 minutes. Remove the cake from pans and cool completely on wire racks.
6. *To make the Mocha Buttercream Icing:*Beat the butter, sugar and cocoa at medium speed with an electric mixer until fluffy.Add the whippedcream and coffee liqueur, beating until smooth.
7. Spread chocolate coffee buttercream icing between layers, on top, and at the sides of the cake.
8. Serve and enjoy.

Strawberry Vanilla Chiffon Cake Recipe

This nice and fluffy cake recipe with strawberries and vanilla frosting is very delicious.

Preparation Time: 20 minutes
Total Time: 1 hour 20 minutes
Yield: 10 servings

Ingredients
1 ¾ all-purpose flour
2 tsp. baking powder
1 tsp. salt
1 ¼ cups granulated sugar

½ cup vegetable oil
6 egg yolks
¾ cup strawberries, pureed in blender
6 egg whites
½ tsp. cream of tartar
1 cup vanilla frosting
1 cup strawberries, sliced, for garnish

Method

1. Preheat oven to 350 F.
2. Mix together baking powder, flour, salt and ½ cup granulated sugar in a large bowl. Add the oil, egg yolks, and pureed strawberries. Stir until just combined.
3. In a separate bowl, beat egg whites and cream of tartar using an electric mixer on medium speed until soft peaks form. Gradually add the remaining ¾ cup granulated sugar. Beat until stiff peaks form. Fold the egg white mixture onto the flour mixture. Pourthe batter into an ungreased 10-inch pan.
4. Bake for 50 to 60 minutes or until a cake tester inserted into the cake

comes out clean. Cool in the pan on wire rack.
5. Spread vanilla frosting on top and at the sides of the cake. Garnish with strawberry slices.
6. Serve and enjoy.

Easy Lemon Chiffon Cake Recipe

Treat yourself and your loved ones with this amazing lemon-flavored chiffon cake!

Preparation Time: 20 minutes
Total Time: 1 hour 20 minutes
Yield: 10 servings

Ingredients

7 eggwhites
1 ½ cup sugar
2 cups all-purpose flour
3 tsp. baking powder

1 tsp. salt
¾ cup water
½ cup canola oil
1 Tbsp. lemon zest, finely grated
2 tsp. pure vanilla extract
½ tsp. cream of tartar

Method

1. Preheat oven to 325 F. Place oven rack in the middle of the oven.
2. Combine sugar, flour, baking powder and salt in a large bowl. In another bowl, whisk the egg yolks, oil, lemon peel water and vanilla. Add to flour mixture and stir until well blended.
3. In a separate bowl, beat eggwhites and cream of tartar using an electric mixer on medium speed until stiff peaks form. Fold gently the egg white mixture into the flour mixture. Pour onto ungreased 9x5x3-inch loaf pan. Bake for 50 to 55 minutes or until cake tester comes out clean. Cool in the pan for 10 minutes. Invert pan onto a wire rack and allow to cool.

4. Serve and enjoy.

Made in the USA
Middletown, DE
11 August 2017